The Atlas of
Famous Battles
of the American
Revolution ™

The Battle of Yorktown

Wendy Vierow

The Rosen Publishing Group's
PowerKids Press ™
New York

To Debbie, my sister

Published in 2003 by The Rosen Publishing Group, Inc.
29 East 21st Street, New York, NY 10010

First Edition

Editor: Nancy MacDonell Smith

Book Design: Michael J. Caroleo

Photo Credits: Cover, title page, pp. 15–16, 19 (maps) by Maria Melendez; cover, title page, pp. 4, 7 (Washington and Cornwallis), 11 (bottom and inset illustrations), 19 (illustration) © North Wind Picture Archives; pp. 4 , 7 (maps) Map Division Library of Congress; pp. 4 (left), 15 (inset right), 16 (illustration) © Culver Pictures; p. 7 (inset), the Emett Collection, Miriam and Ira D. Wallach Division of Art, Prints, and Photographs, New York Public Library, Astor, Lenox, and Tilden Foundations; pp. 8, 20 (map) by Nick Sciacca; p. 8, (far left) © Independence National Historic Park; p. 8 (left) © Archivo Iconografico, S.A./CORBIS; pp. 11–12 (map) © CORBIS; pp. 12 (photo), 16 (cannon) © National Park Service, Colonial National Historical Park; p. 12 (left) Bettmann/CORBIS; p. 15 (inset bottom) Dover Pictoral Archive Series; pp. 16 (bayonet), 19 (rifle) courtesy George C. Neumann Collection, Valley Forge National Historic Park, photos by Cindy Reiman; p. 20 (bottom illustration) © SuperStock; p. 20 (left) © Anne S. K. Brown Military Collection, Brown University Library.

Vierow, Wendy.
The Battle of Yorktown / Wendy Vierow.
    p. cm. – (The Atlas of famous battles of the American Revolution)
Summary: Details the advancement of the British and American troops at the Battle of Yorktown in Virginia in 1781.
Includes bibliographical references and index.
ISBN 0-8239-6331-4 (library binding)
1. Yorktown (Va.)—History—Siege, 1781—Juvenile literature. [1. Yorktown (Va.)—History—Siege, 1781. 2. United States—History—Revolution, 1775–1783—Campaigns.] I. Title. II. Series.
  E241.Y6 V57 2003
  973.3'37—dc21

                                                                            2001007778

Manufactured in the United States of America

Contents

The French king sent soldiers to help the colonists fight the British.

Americans Fight a Revolution

The Battle of Yorktown, fought in the fall of 1781, was the last major battle of the **American Revolution**. Late in the winter of 1779, France gave the United States much-needed money, military equipment, and soldiers to help fight the war against Great Britain. France and the United States were **allies**. With the help of France, Americans stood a better chance of winning the war.

Although French troops had their own French commanders, they were also under the command of American general George Washington, the commander in chief of the **Continental army**. The Continental army, made up of white American and African American soldiers, fought alongside French and German troops at Yorktown. Thanks to France's help, the 17,000 soldiers fighting on the American side outnumbered the 8,300 British, **Hessian**, African American, and white American **loyalists** fighting for the British at Yorktown.

This map of the 13 colonies dates from the time of the American Revolution. The Battle of Yorktown took place in the colony of Virginia. **Bottom Right**: *General George Washington, a Virginian, was a skilled soldier, farmer, businessman, and politician.*

The British Move South

At first the British fought mostly in the northern **colonies**, such as Pennsylvania, New Jersey, and New York. They hoped to win the war by winning battles in the North. When the French joined the Americans in the fight, the British changed their plans. They realized it would be harder to win in the North when the Americans had help. The British decided to fight in the South, where they thought more Americans supported the British king. At first the British did well in the South. However, in the end the British did not find the support they needed. Southerners were angry with the British for destroying property, killing southerners, and promising freedom to slaves who fought for the British.

In 1780, British lieutenant general Charles Cornwallis led troops into the South. The British commander in chief, Sir Henry Clinton, wanted Cornwallis's troops in New York, which he feared General Washington would attack next. However, Cornwallis decided to remain in Virginia.

The British army moved south, because they thought that they would find more support there.
Top Right: *General Sir Henry Clinton was the third British commander in chief since the war started. Earlier commanders in chief were replaced because they could not defeat the Americans.*

Lieutenant General
Charles Cornwallis
was second in
command to
General Clinton.

COLOR KEY

American Troops:

French Troops:

British Regulars:

N

Maryland

Virginia

General Anthony Wayne was a politician from Pennsylvania. He also fought at Brandywine and Monmouth, both in the North.

Gloucester Point

Yorktown

The British Go to Yorktown

Throughout the spring and summer of 1781, General Cornwallis's army fought soldiers commanded by Major General Marquis de Lafayette of France. Lafayette was a French soldier and a politician. During this time, Cornwallis also fought the troops of American brigadier general Anthony Wayne.

In August 1781, Cornwallis and his troops stopped fighting the Americans and the French in Virginia to follow a command by General Clinton. Clinton wanted Cornwallis to create a port for the British fleet on the lower Chesapeake Bay. Cornwallis chose the small town of Yorktown, Virginia, as the location for the port. Yorktown had a harbor on the York River. It also had **fortifications**, but the fortifications were not well laid out. To create an escape route from Yorktown, Cornwallis placed British troops at Gloucester Point, across the York River.

General Cornwallis moved his troops to Yorktown, Virginia. Yorktown was chosen because it was on the water and could be reached by British ships. **Bottom Inset:** *General Lafayette was in his midtwenties when he fought at Yorktown.*

The Americans and the French March South

In August 1781, the same month that General Cornwallis arrived in Yorktown, General Washington learned that a French **fleet** with troops and supplies was sailing for Chesapeake Bay.

Washington and Lafayette realized that the French fleet could prevent Cornwallis's troops at Yorktown from receiving supplies and from escaping by sea. Washington decided to move his troops secretly to Virginia. Marching with Washington's troops were French soldiers under Lieutenant General Jean-Baptiste-Donatien de Vimeur, Comte de Rochambeau. Washington and Rochambeau's troops would join the troops of General Lafayette and General Wayne to fight at Yorktown.

On September 5, 1781, the French fleet fought the British navy near Chesapeake Bay. The French had more ships and fought a better battle than did the British. After winning the battle, the French fleet formed a **blockade** to prevent British ships from aiding Cornwallis at Yorktown.

The French formed a blockade by placing their ships across the entrance to Chesapeake Bay. A few days later, Cornwallis received word from General Clinton in New York that he would send men and supplies to Yorktown. **Top Right**: *The British ship Sharon was destroyed by the French.*

10

Jean-Baptiste-Donatien de Vimeur, Comte de Rochambeau, was an experienced soldier. He worked closely with American officers to help win the war.

Fairfield

Lewis

Mockjack Bay

Rosewel

YORK

Toes Point

JAMES C.ty

Corps d'Hussardes

Corps Americain

uppenhall

Legion de Lauzun

Postes de M.de Choisy

RIVER

Glocester

Fort

Long Island

WILLAMSBURG

Digges

Egg I.

Redoute

Fort

Corps du Marquis
de St. Simon

Redoute

Volontaires de
la Fayette

YORK-TOWN

Reserve de Canons et Morters

Corps de l'armée C.te
de Rochambeau

Parc d'Artillerie

Corps d'Armée du
General Washington

Burwell

Bray

Burwell

YORK COUNTY

Halfway House

Back Bay

Hog I.

ELIZABETH C.ty

Seldon

JAMES

Hampton

CHESAPEAK

This is what one of the redoubts built by the British to defend the road into Yorktown looks like today.

British Troops Leave Their Positions

   On September 28, 1781, American and French troops marched into Yorktown. The Americans set up camp south of Yorktown. The French settled to the north. The next day, the British fired on the Americans and the French, and there was some minor fighting.

   To defend themselves, the British had built 10 small forts, called **redoubts**, around Yorktown. **Trenches** connected the redoubts. On the morning of September 30, 1781, the Americans and the French discovered that the British had left their outermost positions near Yorktown during the night. Expecting 5,000 troops and supplies from General Clinton, General Cornwallis had decided to move his troops nearer to town. By doing this, he hoped to save the lives of his men and to better defend Yorktown until help arrived from Clinton.

   The Americans and the French moved into the positions that the British had abandoned. They were now much closer to Yorktown.

Cornwallis abandoned his outer positions when he realized that his men were outnumbered two to one. **Top Left**: *This engraving shows how a typical American soldier of the time looked.*

The Americans and the French Move In

Once the British left their outermost positions near Yorktown, work was easier for the Americans and the French. They would not have to dig as many trenches as they had planned.

The Americans and the French dug more trenches around Yorktown, in which to place their cannons. The British fired on the allies to try to prevent them from digging. However, the allies kept working. On October 6, 1781, the Americans and the French decided to build a new trench even closer to Yorktown. During the night, the allies quickly dug the trench. In the morning, the British were surprised to find that the allies were even closer to them than they were the day before.

Many of the allies wanted to begin firing on the British. However, Washington told his troops to wait until all the cannons were in place and more trenches were dug. Then the allies would attack full force.

Inset Left: *About 14 soldiers were needed to move and to operate an eighteenth-century cannon.*
Inset Right: *The trenches at Yorktown were dug by hand. The French and American soldiers spent three nights digging all the trenches that were needed.*

The retreat of the British meant that the Americans and the French could move much closer to Yorktown.

General Washington knew that his men must get as close as possible to Yorktown for the battle to be successful. He did not want to give the British any chances to get away.

Yorktown

Gloucester Point

N

COLOR KEY
American Troops:
French Troops:
British Regulars:

This is a cannon from the battle at Yorktown

This bayonet is the kind the French used to capture the redoubt.

The French first cut down the spikes around Redoubt No. 9, then captured it by fighting the British hand to hand. The attack took 30 minutes.

COLOR KEY
American Troops:
French Troops:
British Regulars:

N

The Americans and the French Surround the British

Finally the Americans and the French were ready to fight. On October 9, 1781, at 3:00 P.M., the French fired cannons at the British. Two hours later, the Americans fired their cannons. The guns fired on the British all night and into the next day. General Cornwallis sent messages to General Clinton, asking for help. His supplies were running low.

The allies built another trench even closer to Yorktown. To surround the British, the Americans and the French would have to capture two British redoubts. The French planned to capture Redoubt No. 9, and the Americans would capture Redoubt No. 10.

On the night of October 14, 1781, the Americans and the French attacked and captured the redoubts. During the fight, 9 Americans and 15 French soldiers died. The exact number of British and Hessian deaths is unclear, but it was higher than those on the American side. American and French troops now surrounded the British.

The Americans and the French planned to surround the British, then to take control of Yorktown.

British Troops Try to Escape

Still waiting for help from General Clinton, General Cornwallis knew that he could not hold out much longer. In the early morning of October 16, 1781, Cornwallis ordered his soldiers to ruin American and French guns and cannons. However, the Americans and the French drove them off and repaired the cannons quickly. By dawn they were once again firing at the British. Surrounded and outnumbered, Cornwallis ordered his troops to cross the York River to the town of Gloucester Point, Virginia, where more British troops waited. Late on the night of October 16, the British began to cross the river in boats. Escape would not be easy. The Americans and the French surrounded the British at Gloucester Point. A storm hit and destroyed many British boats. The attempt to reach Gloucester Point failed. Cornwallis ordered his troops to return to Yorktown. By daybreak on October 17, the allies were again firing on the British. Out of **ammunition**, the British could not continue the fight.

18

General Cornwallis knew that an attack on the Americans and the French would fail, so he tried to move his men across the York River to Gloucester Point.

Yorktown

Gloucester
Point

N

COLOR KEY
American Troops:
French Troops:
British Regulars:

Many American soldiers carried rifles. This type of gun worked well, but it had no place on which to attach a bayonet.

The allies fired on the British as the British returned to Yorktown on the morning of October 17, 1781.

Gloucester
Point

N

Yorktown

Drummers were very important in eighteenth-century armies. Different beats told soldiers when to advance and when to retreat.

The British Lose the Battle

At about 10:00 A.M. on October 17, 1781, a British drummer and an officer holding a white flag approached the American and French lines. They carried a note from General Cornwallis for General Washington. Cornwallis wanted to **surrender**.

After one and one-half days of discussion, the two generals agreed on the terms of surrender. British soldiers would become prisoners. British officers would be **paroled** and returned to Great Britain, under the condition that they would not fight in the war again.

At 2:00 P.M. on October 19, 1781, Cornwallis surrendered. That same day General Clinton finally sent British troops to help him. Clinton was too late. The Battle of Yorktown was finished. During the battle, 156 British and Hessian soldiers had been killed and 326 had been wounded. The Americans and the French lost 72 soldiers. There were 190 wounded American and French soldiers.

The British troops marched toward the Americans and the French to surrender. **Bottom:** *The American troops flew the Stars and Stripes during the surrender at Yorktown.*

21

The Revolution Ends

Early on the morning of October 24, 1781, news of the surrender reached America's leaders in Philadelphia, Pennsylvania. The city celebrated with fireworks, bells, and parties.

When news of the surrender reached Great Britain in late November, it became clear that the war was pretty much finished. The British people were tired of fighting. Clinton was relieved of his command. Many British **citizens** blamed Clinton for Britain's loss at Yorktown, because he had been too slow in helping Cornwallis.

The Battle of Yorktown did not end the American Revolution. However, it was the last major battle of the war. The fighting continued for two more years.

Before a peace **treaty** could be signed, Great Britain and the United States had many details to discuss, such as the new country's borders. Finally on September 3, 1783, Great Britain and the United States signed a peace treaty. The United States of America was now a free country.

Glossary

allies (A-lyz) Countries that support one another.

American Revolution (uh-MER-uh-ken reh-vuh-LOO-shun) Battles that soldiers from the American colonies fought against Britain for freedom, from 1775 to 1783.

ammunition (am-yoo-NIH-shun) Things fired from weapons, such as bullets.

blockade (blah-KAYD) Ships that block the passage of other ships into ports of another country.

citizens (SIH-tih-zenz) People who are born in or have a legal right to live in a country.

colonies (KAH-luh-neez) New places to where people, who are still ruled by the old country's leaders, move.

Continental army (kon-tin-EN-tul AR-mee) The army of patriots created in 1775, with George Washington as its commander in chief.

fleet (FLEET) Many ships under the command of one person.

fortifications (for-tih-fih-KAY-shunz) Strong buildings or places that can be defended against an enemy.

Hessian (HEH-shen) A German soldier who was paid to fight for the British during the American Revolution.

loyalists (LOY-uh-lists) People who are loyal to a certain political party, government, or ruler.

paroled (puh-ROHLD) To have released a prisoner on the condition that the person act according to the law.

redoubts (rih-DOWTS) Small forts outside fortifications to defend the gates.

surrender (suh-REN-der) To give up a fight or battle.

treaty (TREE-tee) A formal agreement, signed and agreed upon by each party.

trenches (TREN-chez) Long pits dug in the ground, where soldiers hid to shoot at an enemy.

Index

Primary Sources

Cover, page 4. *George Washington.* This hand-colored engraving is based on a 1772 oil painting by Charles Willson Peale, which is in the collection of Washington and Lee University, Lexington, Virginia. In this engraving, Washington wears the British militia uniform of the 22nd Regiment of Virginia. Washington had left the militia in 1758. By wearing his uniform in this portrait, he was letting the British know that he was ready to fight for his country. The American Revolution would not start for several years but already people were unhappy with British rule. **Pages 4, 7, 11, 12.** *A Map of the British and French Dominions in North America. John Mitchell, c. 1774.* Map Division of the Library of Congress. This map was drafted by a man named John Mitchell and printed by Jeffreys and Faden, a company in London. Jeffreys and Faden were geographers to King George III, and made many maps for him. **Page 8 (left).** *Major General Anthony Wayne.* Oil on canvas, Charles Willson Peale, 1783. This portrait was made when Wayne was 38 years old. Charles Willson Peale also painted other famous Americans, including Martha Washington, Benjamin Franklin, and Alexander Hamilton. **Page 12 (bottom).** *Redoubt.* This redoubt was originally dug by the British and was captured by the colonists during the Battle of Yorktown. During the 1930s, this and other redoubts at Yorktown were recreated by the Civilian Conservation Corps (CCC). The CCC recreated this redoubt so that modern-day Americans would know what the Battle of Yorktown had been like. **Page 20 (bottom).** *The Surrender of Cornwallis.* Oil on canvas, John Trumbull, 1820. Collection of the Office of the Architect of the Capitol. In 1789, John Trumbull wrote to Thomas Jefferson, "The greatest motive I had or have for continuing in my pursuit of painting has been the wish of commemorating the great events of our country's Revolution." Trumbull had been a colonel in the Continental army, so he knew first hand what battle was like. He painted many scenes from the American Revolution, four of which hang in the U.S. Capitol Rotunda. This painting is one of Trumbull's most famous works.

Web Sites

Due to the changing nature of Internet links, PowerKids Press has developed an online list of Web sites related to the topic of this book. This site is updated regularly. Please use this link to access the list:

www.powerkidslinks.com/afbar/yorktown/